THE HEROIC LEADERSHIP WORKBOOK

I0810473

THE HEROIC LEADERSHIP WORKBOOK

CHRIS LOWNEY

WITH JUDY WEARING

LOYOLA PRESS.
A JESUIT MINISTRY

Unless otherwise noted, the quotations cited in this workbook are taken from the paperback edition of *Heroic Leadership: Best Practices from a 450-Year-Old Company that Changed the World* (Loyola Press, 2003).

LOYOLA PRESS.
A JESUIT MINISTRY

www.loyolapress.com

Copyright © 2025 by Chris Lowney and Judy Wearing
All rights reserved.

Cover art credits: in8finity/Getty Images

ISBN: 978-0-8294-5715-5
Library of Congress Control Number: 2024950178

Published in Chicago, IL
Printed in the United States of America
24 25 26 27 28 29 30 31 32 33 Versa 10 9 8 7 6 5 4 3 2 1

CONTENTS

WELCOME

TO THIS 30-DAY WORKBOOK EXPERIENCE IN HEROIC LEADERSHIP!

The Heroic Leadership Workbook is a workbook to accompany my book *Heroic Leadership: Best Practices from a 450-Year-Old Company That Changed the World.* That book explored the early Jesuits' remarkable history and made the case that those Jesuits thrived (and still thrive) in part because of a culture that prized self-awareness, heroism, ingenuity, and love as four foundational pillars of what we know as leadership. Such leadership is heroic when it enables and empowers leaders to transcend themselves and their egos to serve missions that inspire their allegiance, excellence, and imagination.

If that book was largely about the Jesuits, this companion workbook is about you and your call to heroic leadership, whatever your stage of life, whether you are a student or a retiree, and whatever your life pursuits, whether you are managing hundreds of people or simply managing your own life. The exercises that follow will guide you through a carefully crafted, spiritual, reflective journey. You will emerge with a deeper understanding of yourself, your values, your characteristic ways of engaging colleagues, and how all of these things impact your leadership effectiveness. You will also be invited (or, put another way, challenged) to connect your deepest personal and spiritual beliefs to your everyday life and the work you do in order to cultivate a life that is wholly integrated rather than fragmented. By the end of the workbook experience, you will be able to articulate with clarity and confidence: *This is who I am. This is the leadership statement I will make with my life. This is what I will change. And this is what I will do more often.*

Thanks for joining me in the journey to heroic leadership.

—Chris

"We can be leaders in everything we do—in our work and in our daily lives, when teaching others or learning from others. And most of us do all those things in the course of any given day."

HOW TO GET THE MOST OUT OF THIS WORKBOOK EXPERIENCE

Heroic Leadership is grounded in Jesuit spirituality, most especially as it was laid out in Ignatius of Loyola's masterwork, *The Spiritual Exercises of Saint Ignatius* (see chapter 6 in *Heroic Leadership*), which is comprised of not just text to be read, but of a series of exercises to be done.

So it is with this workbook. If all you do is read through the following exercises, you will have wasted your precious time. What you get out of it will match what you put into it, and the workbook experience will bear great fruit if you invest enough reflective time to learn or clarify something about yourself from each exercise. Please work through the exercises steadily, dedicating, if possible, a bit of time each day for thirty consecutive days.

However, don't think of these exercises as if you are training for a race, where you build up stamina by going faster and faster. If anything, it's the opposite: a great mantra of Jesuit spirituality is to "pause where you find fruit." Please do just that! If one particular exercise really gets you thinking, and you want to mull it over for another day before moving to the next one, go right ahead and do so.

If a prayerful or spiritual routine is already part of your life, I strongly encourage you to bring the questions posed in these exercises to your prayer life. By doing so, you'll achieve one of this workbook's core goals: to pursue a "whole" life—that is, work and lead and live in a way that integrates your deepest spiritual and religious beliefs into your work and human interactions, and you will conquer the modern disease of "split-life-ism," where you set aside your authentic self and values every morning in order to become a different "work self" in your company or organization.

Finally, while this workbook draws faithfully from my book *Heroic Leadership*, it does not do so in a linear fashion. In other words, this workbook is not intended to be used side-by-side with the book as you read it from beginning to end. Rather, this workbook reflects a more organic rhythm, inviting you to reflect on leadership themes as they pertain to your day-to-day experience.

Readers who want to undertake these workbook exercises as part of a cohort in a university-credentialed certificate program have two wonderful opportunities to do so. See page 70 of this workbook for more information.

I wish you the very best as you go forward, and I'll be happy to hear what you learn from the workbook experience. I'm easy to find at www.chrislowney.com.

—Chris Lowney

"As I considered Ignatius Loyola and his early Jesuit colleagues, I became convinced that their approach to molding innovative, risk-taking, ambitious, flexible global thinkers worked. In some ways—dare I say—it worked better than many modern corporate efforts to do the same."

A CALL TO HEROIC LEADERSHIP

A plethora of leadership books are churned out every year, often by sports stars or celebrity-CEOs who are implicitly pitching a promise ("Here's how you, too, can reach the pinnacle of success!"). Well, such advice may help the infinitesimal minority who are clawing their way to the top, but what about the rest of us? We're essentially marginalized in the leadership discussion, gazing up at the high and mighty.

My book *Heroic Leadership* staked out a radically different claim: namely, that every one of us has a leadership opportunity and responsibility, a calling to show leadership. Not if we someday become pope or a corporate titan, but *right now,* whether we are high school students or retirees, whether we labor in corporations, in schools, or at home.

That's not a rhetorical gimmick. Dictionary definitions highlight the pointing out of a way and the act of influencing people toward a goal as signs of leadership. Well, we're each pointing a way all the time. How we treat others, what we prioritize, and the values we model all point out a "way": our leadership statement about how humans ought to treat one another, our proclamation of what's worthy of time, effort, and sacrifice.

Trouble is, many of us have never deliberately pondered the leadership statement that our lives are making. Only by becoming more intentional can we flourish and realize our potential. And, by becoming what we can be, we'll help society become what it *should* be.

The following exercises crack open this idea that "everyone leads." We'll ponder our current life trajectory as leaders, and we'll consider how we might want to fine-tune that trajectory to become the best leaders we can be.

"We're all leaders, and we're leading all the time, well or poorly."

DAY 1: LIVING LEADERS

Chapter 4 in *Heroic Leadership* addresses leadership role models. Think of the names of several living leaders that you consider to be leadership role models. Write down their names in the chart below.

Then, think about why such names came to mind. What qualities or characteristics do you associate with each person? What makes someone a good leader?

NAME OF LEADER	QUALITIES OR CHARACTERISTICS

Re-read your list of qualities that characterize good leaders. Chances are, many of the qualities on your list are qualities that you yourself could embody, no? This simple exercise validates the claim that we're all leading; that is, we all have daily opportunities to model the qualities that we associate with good leadership.

"Leadership is not merely getting the job done; it's how the job is done."

HOW ARE YOU A LEADER?

As we learn in chapter 5 in *Heroic Leadership*, self-awareness is the foundation of leadership. Let's engage in some self-awareness.

In the first column on the chart below, brainstorm times in the past few days or weeks when you've had an opportunity to influence others. In other words, think of times when you've been given a chance to lead, like it or not. Fill out this column first.

Then, in the second column, beside each opportunity, assess how well you answered the opportunity. Did you respond well? Or did you do a less-than-ideal job of leading?

In the third column, alongside opportunities to influence others that you feel you could have done better, consider what you might learn from your less-than-stellar contribution. For example, what do you think held you back? What might you do differently next time?

OPPORTUNITY TO LEAD	HOW DID I RESPOND?	WHAT DID I LEARN?

"The good news is that everyone has the capacity to cultivate leadership skills by committing to the personal introspective investment that will develop them."

DAY 2: MY CAREER JOURNEY

Chapter 2 in *Heroic Leadership* explains that "[Ignatius's] journey to company leadership provokes reflection on the attributes that distinguish true leadership." Let's take a look at your own career and life journey thus far.

Visualize your life as a journey or a timeline. You may use the timeline template provided on page 14 of this workbook, or create your own on paper or by using your favorite software. Write down the events, turning points, and big learning moments over the years that have led you to be where you are in your:

- professional life
- personal life
- current position
- principal pursuits

These are the crossroads that constitute your career story. Events and milestones in your personal life may or may not have played a large role.

> **NOTE:** Do not overthink this or spend a lot of time being thorough. You can always come back and add to your timeline as you reflect further on your life. In fact, we will be referring back to this timeline as we proceed through the workbook.

REFLECTION

Once you have completed your timeline or map, circle the event(s) or milestone(s) that were most impactful. In the box below, jot down your initial thoughts about these impactful events and milestones.

- What did you learn?
- In what ways were you changed?
- Did your goals shift and, if so, how?

"Leadership is defined not by the scale of the opportunity but by the quality of the response."

On your timeline, draw a line under any events that you consider negative—events that might evoke negative emotions, shame, or the desire to avoid thinking about them. Draw a box around any events you consider positive.

Identify any additional positive events or negative events in your journey.

What were the main consequences of the negative events?

How did you respond to the negative events?

Overall, what did you learn and how did you grow from these events?

"The measure of [early explorers'] personal greatness is less what they found at journey's end and more the depth of human character that carried them along the way, [including] willingness to bear the risk of failure."

MY LIFE AND CAREER JOURNEY TIMELINE TEMPLATE

SELF-AWARENESS

Ignatius of Loyola didn't imagine our mentors or spiritual advisors as all-seeing gurus who gaze into our depths and utter profound insights. Rather, he said, a good guide should "point, as with the finger, to the vein in the mine, and let each one dig for himself." Think of the following exercises as "pointers," each indicating some "vein in the mine" where self-reflection might bear fruit. It's surely worth the effort: you can't lead others credibly unless you can lead yourself, and you can't lead yourself without knowing yourself. Self-awareness (the focus of chapter 5 in *Heroic Leadership*) begins with a foundational investment: inventorying your strengths, weaknesses, values, and characteristic ways of behaving, especially self-sabotaging habits. But the best leaders go deeper, wrestling with life's big questions: What's my deeper purpose and sense of mission? What do we humans inherently owe to each other and society, and how should we treat one another? For many of us, the answers to these big questions will draw from our faith tradition.

This foundational investment must in turn be complemented with tools for staying on track and understanding what's going on inside us amid the challenges, changing circumstances, stress, and distractions of each day. Accordingly, Day 6's exercise will introduce the Jesuit *examen*; this mental and spiritual pit stop from each day's chaotic pace is a precious chance to take stock, remind yourself of what's important, and cultivate a spirit of gratitude (see p. 124 in *Heroic Leadership*).

The week's final exercise (Day 9) will challenge you to ruminate on some crisis or challenge that you've faced, what Jesuits sometimes call a "cannonball moment," referencing the severe battle injury that shattered Ignatius of Loyola's leg as well as his life plans, engendering his profound reassessment and conversion (see chapter 3, "The Jesuits," in *Heroic Leadership*). Though few of us have endured such trauma, all of us have faced inflection points, whether moments of great joy (like a child's birth) or wrenching disappointment (like a lost job or relationship). The week's final blessing will be to ponder what such moments have taught you as a leader.

"No one can make another person self-aware, so leaders must largely mold themselves. Only I can muster the will, courage, and honesty to search myself."

DAY 3: WHAT DO YOU VALUE?

The next page lists a number of common values. Take a few minutes to choose your top twelve values that intuitively are most important in your life and write them here. If there's an important value that isn't included on the list, feel free to add it.

1.		**7.**	
2.		**8.**	
3.		**9.**	
4.		**10.**	
5.		**11.**	
6.		**12.**	

Chapter 11 in *Heroic Leadership* explores the concept of core values. Your core values are the values that are of utmost importance to you. To get at your core values, look at your list above and cross out six that are easiest for you to "give up." Of the six remaining core values, list the three that are of the utmost importance. Can you rank them in order of importance?

1.	
2.	
3.	

After completing the above task, some people have a revelation about what is most important to them. Others are not surprised at all. While you are thinking about it, jot down how your behavior in your professional life manifests your core values.

"Key to attaining self-awareness is identifying motivating core values and beliefs."

LIST OF COMMON VALUES

Family	Freedom	Security	Harmony
Loyalty	Intelligence	Connection	Self-respect
Humanity	Success	Enjoyment	Invention
Diversity	Generosity	Integrity	Finesse
Love	Openness	Spirituality	Order
Advancement	Respect	Joy/Play	Certainty
Work ethic	Excitement	Change	Goodness
Involvement	Faith	Wisdom	Beauty
Caring	Personal development	This too shall pass	Honesty
Adventure	Kindness	Teamwork	Safety
Communication	Learning	Excellence	Innovation
Quality	Commonality	Contributing	Spiritualism
Strength	Entertain	Wealth	Speed
Power	Affection	Cooperation	Peace
Friendship	Encouragement	Pride in your work	Clarity
Fun	Charisma	Humor	Leadership
Renewal	Home	Fidelity	Contentment
Abundance	Courage	Balance	Compassion
Fitness	Professionalism	Relationship	Knowledge
Happiness	Change	Prosperity	Wellness
Finances	Gratitude	Grace	Endurance
Facilitation	Effectiveness	Reciprocity	Fame
Entrepreneurial	Justice	Appreciation	Willingness
Patience	Giving people a chance	Forgiveness	Creativity

DAY 4: LOOKING BACK AT YOUR LIFE JOURNEY

With chapter 11, "The Way We Do Things," in mind, review your My Life and Career Journey timeline that you completed on Day 2, and reflect on how your strengths, weaknesses, values, and purpose connect to the events and turning points in your life and career.

PART 1: STRENGTHS AND WEAKNESSES

Reflect on the events you've included in your timeline. How would you describe your strengths, and how did you exhibit them in your reactions to these events? Circle or highlight the descriptions of strengths below that resonate with you.

NOTE: You don't need to stick to this list; if strengths come to mind that are not on this list, include them!

Ambitious	Good negotiator	Logical
Persistent	Enthusiastic	Compliant
Networking	Team player	Detail-oriented
Authentic	Convincing	Motivated
Responsible	Flexible	Analytical
Problem-solving	Strives for excellence	Interpersonal skills
Caring	Well-organized	Optimistic
Self-controlled	Honest	Invites challenge
Creative	Leadership	Likeable
Trustworthy	Loyal	Open-minded
Effective listener	Integrity	Time management
Dedicated	Good communicator	Independent
Versatile	Able to delegate	Tenacity

My core strengths:

On your timeline, alongside the key events, write the strengths you used in handling the challenges.

"By figuring out what he or she is good at, stands for, and wants in life, the leader positions him- or herself to choose a career and a lifestyle that draw on those strengths, values, and goals."

Continuing with the focus on chapter 11, look over the following list, which prompts you to think about your core weaknesses. Reflect on the events in your timeline. Consider what you have done as well as the things you have failed to do. Circle or highlight what you consider to be your core weaknesses. As in the exercise on the previous page, feel free to list weaknesses that do not appear on this list.

> **NOTE:** You don't need to stick to this list; if weaknesses come to mind that are not on this list, include them!

Defensive	Impatient	Lazy	Easily bored
Procrastinate	Give up easily	Take things personally	Strong-willed
Passive	Conflict aversive	Shy	Disloyal
Poor long-term planning	Inflexible	Short-sighted	Selfish
Focuses on small details	Takes blame for others	Too outspoken	Greedy
Too self-reliant	Needs to be right	Stubborn	Does not multitask
Poor emotional regulation	Controlling	Poor communication	Impulsive
Bossy	Takes on too much	Lack of follow-through	Aggressive
Takes big risks	Critical of others	Does not see big picture	Work-life imbalance
Perfectionist	Fearful	Self-critical	Has trouble in teams
Closed-minded	Disorganized	Does not like pressure	Blames others
Lack of empathy	Low emotional intelligence	Lack of self-awareness	Judgmental

In the list above, circle your core weaknesses.

Beside key events on your timeline, jot down the weaknesses you displayed in handling these challenges.

"Only those who have pinpointed their weaknesses can conquer them."

PART 2: VALUES AND PURPOSE

Chapter 3 in *Heroic Leadership* focuses on having a "purposeful vision." Consider why you made the decisions you made along your life path. This reflection might help to uncover the values you've held dear, and the purpose that's been motivating you.

One or two of the biggest decisions I made in response to opportunities and challenges I have faced are:

The big decisions I made in response to opportunities and challenges I have faced suggest that what I value most in my life is:

When I reflect on the decisions I made in response to the opportunities and challenges I have faced, what I'd like to change about myself is:

"In the end, the leader's values keep his or her life feeling 'pulled together' in a complex world."

DAY 5: UNIQUE PURPOSE BRAINSTORM

Continuing the focus on purposeful vision (chapter 3 in *Heroic Leadership*), quickly skim the scenarios below and on the next page. Choose three that draw you in or speak to you most powerfully to go back to and answer.

You can do these thought experiments in your head, but writing can be more effective in evoking your imagination. Jot some notes in the second column about what your thinking and writing suggests about your core purpose.

THOUGHT EXPERIMENT	WHAT DOES MY THINKING SAY ABOUT MY PURPOSE AND PRINCIPLES?
UNIQUE TALENTS: Think of what others have told you about the impact you have had on them. What do you get told repeatedly about how you influence others? For example, are you motivating or convincing? Do you teach, give comfort, generate ideas, or help solve problems?	
YOUR BEST FUTURE: Imagine you are free to do whatever you would like to do in life. Imagine it is five years in the future and you get a phone call from a friend. Your friend says, "Hello! So good to talk to you. How is it going? What are you up to? Are you flourishing in your life? What is it about your life that contributes to your flourishing?" How will you respond to these questions?	
YOUR CHILDHOOD DREAMS: Imagine a younger version of yourself before the adult responsibilities of a job, family, and caring for others became primary activities for you. Maybe you were fourteen, five, or even younger when you were carefree. Maybe they were fleeting moments. Maybe they were sustained durations. Either way, imagine yourself back then in those carefree moments. What are you wearing? What expressions are on your face? What emotions are you feeling? Have a discussion with your younger self. Imagine the conversation as you ask your younger self: What do you want in life? What are your deepest talents? What impact will you have on others, including your loved ones, at work, at home, and in the world? What kind of person do you feel called to be in life? What is your purpose in life? For what should you live?	

YOUR EULOGY: imagine your funeral and the people gathered around. What do you hope they say about you? How will you live your life consistently from this moment forward in order to evoke your ideal eulogy?	
IMPORTANT TEACHINGS: What writings, teachings, or religious beliefs have most resonated with you throughout your life? What is it about these writings or teachings that resonates so intensely?	
YOUR MANTRA: If you had a mantra that represents your "life philosophy," what would it be?	
YOUR ELEVATOR PITCH: write a three-minute elevator pitch that describes who you are and what you're about.	
YOUR CORE VALUES: look at your top three values (refer to the value-sorting exercise you completed on Day 3). What are some ways these values manifest in your actions? In other words, according to your core values, what kind of person do you feel called to be in life? For what should you live?	

"The leader understands that his or her values and ways of working must form an integrated, self-reinforcing whole, or as Jesuits called it, a *modo de proceder* (a way of proceeding)."

DAY 6: DAILY SELF-AWARENESS

An entire lesson in this unit is devoted to practicing a daily self-awareness routine. Based on St. Ignatius of Loyola's notion of a daily *examen* (see pp. 124–126 in *Heroic Leadership*), the practice allows you to pay attention and adjust what's going on "in the inside." The details of the routine can be personalized in ways that make it more likely you'll actually do it. Here are some guiding steps and ideas to help you decide what you might do to incorporate a daily self-awareness routine into your own life. Highlight, circle, or put a checkmark beside those that will work best for you.

TAKE ACTION

Here are some ideas for how you can break free from distraction to engage in a self-awareness routine.

HOW?

- ☐ While doing routine tasks at home or work
- ☐ Add to already existing relaxation routines
- ☐ Close my eyes and think
- ☐ Keep a notebook
- ☐ Make a voice recording on my phone
- ☐ Use an app
- ☐ Other: ____________________

WHERE?

- ☐ On the job
- ☐ At the desk
- ☐ In the break room
- ☐ On the commute home
- ☐ Lying down to sleep (nap/night)
- ☐ While exercising
- ☐ While taking a walk
- ☐ Other: ____________________

WHEN?

- ☐ On a formal break
- ☐ During meals
- ☐ While doing home upkeep
- ☐ Exercise time
- ☐ During your daily prayer time
- ☐ Other: ____________________

HOW WILL YOU REMIND YOURSELF TO DO IT?

- ☐ Use an app
- ☐ Put it in my calendar
- ☐ Scheduled emails to myself
- ☐ Reminders on my phone
- ☐ Post-it notes in my chosen location
- ☐ Other: ____________________

"Self-awareness is never a finished product."

WHAT WILL YOU DO OR SAY TO YOURSELF IF YOU FORGET?

- Create a reminder
- Commit to doing it the next day by telling someone else my intent or write it down
- Recognize it takes a while to establish a new habit and keep trying
- Other: ______________________

What will you think about? Here are some ideas.

GRATITUDE

What am I especially grateful for today?

- The love and support I received by . . .
- The courage I mustered to . . .
- An event that took place today . . .

BIRD'S-EYE VIEW

- What are my life priorities?
- What is my core purpose?
- What is my calling?

TAKING STOCK

- In what ways have I done well as a leader today?
- What about today troubles me?
- What has challenged me today?
- How did I respond?

The IgnatianSpirituality.com website includes an *Examen* page with wonderful spiritual resources and pointers for this practice. Or, you can consult non-religious resources such as:

Chains.cc
chains.cc

Uses a calendar and a powerful metaphor to help keep you motivated to work every day toward new habits.

Todoist
Todoist.com

An organizer's dream with lots of features, including prioritizing, delegating, and visual progress reports.

DAY 7: GRATITUDE

YOUR COLLEAGUES

Write the first names of people in the first column, then describe why you are grateful for each person.

NAME	GRATEFUL BECAUSE

Take a look at what you've written above. What do you notice about the people you are grateful for?

"Each *examen* begins by recalling the positive, loving worldview that was the Exercises' culminating meditation: 'The First Point is to give thanks to God our Lord for the benefits I have received.'"

TAKE ACTION

EXPRESS YOUR GRATITUDE

Consider expressing your gratitude directly to some or all of your colleagues, family, friends, neighbors, and people you interact with as you go about your life. This could be via email, text, social media, phone, or in person, depending on how you typically interact with the person.

For example, you might say, "Dear Joe: Thank you for coming to my rescue and pitching in on that project when I was totally overwhelmed with the workload." Or, "Marie: Thank you for your understanding when my kid was sick and I had to scoot off now and then."

REFLECTION

Research demonstrates that the expression of gratitude improves mood. The next day, after expressing your gratitude, take a moment to reflect on how it felt.

Did expressing your gratitude influence your mood?

Do you have any evidence to suggest whether your words had an impact?

Do you regularly express your gratitude to others? If not, why not?

"Appreciating himself as a loved person of unique dignity and potential inevitably affects the way [one] lives his life, instilling in him the desire to make the most of his gifts."

DAY 8: *MAGIS*-DRIVEN LEADERSHIP

As I explained in *Heroic Leadership*, *magis*-driven leadership stands apart from all other types of leadership. In the Ignatian tradition, *magis* means that we strive toward God's greater glory in everything we do. Whatever your spiritual tradition may be, you can understand *magis* as an ongoing commitment to develop one's gifts to the fullest for purposes that transcend one's own selfish desires.

This exercise guides you through this thought process; it can be deeply impactful, but also deeply thought-provoking. Be brave!

YOUR BEST LIFE

Imagine yourself living your best life. Imagine yourself walking through the door into your home after a day of work, community activities, or school.

- What do you see?
- Who is there?
- What photographs are on the walls or mantle?
- What have you been doing?
- What will you do for the rest of the day?
- What challenges have you faced that day?
- How do you feel?
- What is your physical, mental, and emotional energy level?

Now, imagine looking down at yourself in the life you are living now.

- What kind of life are you actually living?
- What is preventing you from living your best possible life?
- Are these obstacles natural or self-imposed? Do they really exist?

REFLECTION

Think about each aspect of your current life and fill out the following chart with what it might look like based on your imagined best life.

ASPECT OF WORK/LIFE	WHAT PURSUING YOUR BEST LIFE LOOKS LIKE
The tasks that I perform in the course of my day	
My interactions with colleagues	
My interactions with those we serve	
Fulfillment of my life's purpose	
Enactment of my core values in my work or other pursuits	
Other	

TAKE ACTION

After thinking about what it means to be living your best life, write a sentence or a statement to help fortify your decision to live according to your purpose and your values.

I decide to . . .

"Heroic leadership invites us to replace accidental leadership with purposeful leadership, of self and others."

DAY 9: YOUR LEADERSHIP CRUCIBLE

We're now going to try to extract more wisdom and learnings from your major inflection points, challenges, and crises as a leader, keeping in mind that you are a leader because you influence others, whether formally or informally. You might want to revisit your My Life and Career Journey timeline from Day 2 to help remind you of key moments as you work through the following questions.

Those familiar with the Jesuit tradition sometimes refer to these as "cannonball moments," referencing that iconic moment in Ignatius of Loyola's life when a severe battle injury caused by a cannonball forced him into a deep consideration of his own life purpose and direction (see chapter 3 in *Heroic Leadership*, "The Jesuits").

Jot down a few of the biggest moments of crisis/challenge you have experienced.

Regardless of what you understood at the time, look back with fresh eyes now. Ask yourself:

- What do you now understand that you learned from your crisis/challenge?
- What do you now understand about yourself?
- What do you now understand about yourself as a leader?

"Leaders innovate by approaching their challenges in ways their predecessors never imagined."

Crises and challenges often influence our future selves.

- How was your life changed by what happened and your response to it?
- What commitments did you make?
- What priorities and principles did you develop and maintain as a consequence?

TAKE ACTION

Whether or not you made new commitments or developed new principles at the time you faced crises and challenges, you can do so now based on the newfound understanding that comes from reflecting on past experiences. What commitments or insights would you like to take forward with you?

"As the early Jesuits navigated life's rapidly flowing, uncharted, winding waters, even sound navigational principles couldn't help them solve every problem. Insoluble problems emerged, as did dilemmas that had no attractive solutions."

INGENUITY

I typically begin leadership presentations by asking people if they think life has grown more complex, uncertain, and faster paced. Invariably, 90 percent of hands shoot up, whether in Milwaukee or Manila, whether among techies or teachers.

All that change and complexity forces lots of difficult decisions upon us as we face an uncertain, volatile future. This makes ingenuity (the focus of chapter 7 in *Heroic Leadership*) imperative—that is, we need to become hopeful, optimistic leaders whose decision-making prowess enables us to adapt confidently rather than shrink fearfully from what lurks around life's next corner.

My own ingenuity crash course began with a work assignment to J.P. Morgan's Japan office (see chapter 1 in *Heroic Leadership*). It was my crazily distorted reenactment of Francis Xavier's arrival in Japan exactly 433 years before me. Granted, I flew in business class; he endured a treacherous ocean voyage.

As I struggled to adapt to Japanese business culture, I sometimes wondered how that Jesuit had pioneered such a highly adaptive, deeply moral, visionary approach to that unfamiliar environment. Then the light bulb went off: freedom from and freedom for! Of course that was the key. Let me explain.

Freedom from: Ignatius of Loyola brilliantly grasped that our choice-making often drifts off course even before we make choices, because we're subtly haunted by deep-seated fears, self-absorbed drives, and dysfunctional tendencies. So, we might refrain from changing our life for the better not because we can't figure out new paths but because fear holds us back from taking them. Or, we drift into immoral choices not because we're ignorant of what's right, but because inner demons like greed or pride lure us astray. We'll become more ingenious leaders by scrutinizing and setting aside such inner baggage in order for our best selves to take charge of our choices and life direction.

And freedom for? Well, freedom from our inner baggage must be freedom for something, and we're freeing ourselves for loving, heroic leadership, as the following weeks will explore.

"Ingenuity blossoms when the personal freedom to pursue opportunities is linked to a profound trust and optimism that the world presents plenty of them."

DAY 10: YOUR INGENUITY PATTERNS

Continuing with the focus on ingenuity (chapter 7 in *Heroic Leadership*), look back at the life timeline that you created on Day 2. In this exercise, you'll reflect on the decisions you made associated with the key events.

By exploring your past pattern of decisions, you'll become more aware of your decision-making tendencies and your strengths, as well as aspects of decision-making that pose challenges to your fulfillment in work and life.

This exercise will help you begin to pinpoint your decision-making strengths as well as uncover some of the derailing unfreedoms or baggage that may be getting in the way of making great choices.

TYPE OF DECISION	POSITIVE DECISIONS	MISTAKES
Where in your story were there crossroads when it could have gone one way or another? Jot down the best and worst decisions you made.		
What was a major consequence of these decisions on yourself, others, or both?		
As you think back over your life and career crossroads, what did you decide NOT to do?		
What do you imagine are the consequences—for yourself and others—of the decisions you did not make?		
Are there particular fears or biases that crop up when you make big choices? Do you take risks? If so, how big a risk?		

"Jesuit ingenuity is the ability to innovate, to absorb new perspectives, to respond quickly to opportunities or threats, and to let go of strategies that no longer work in order to embrace new ones."

REFLECTION

Read over the chart you filled in on the previous page and make some conclusions.

What patterns do you discern in your positive decisions with respect to your decision-making behavior?

What patterns or characteristic missteps do you discern in your mistakes with respect to your decision-making behavior?

How ingenious have you been throughout your life? Do you keep "one foot raised" and respond to change by embracing opportunity?

** HOW'S YOUR DAILY *EXAMEN* GOING? **

Did you remember to do it today? If not, take three minutes now and reflect on:

- What you're grateful for
- The bird's-eye view of your bigger goals/purpose
- What you've done and who you have been so far today

"By looking at the future with optimism, one becomes more likely to find opportunities and solutions. Loyola called it 'living with one foot raised.'"

DAY 11: THE BAGGAGE CAROUSEL

We're using the colloquial phrase *inner baggage* to paraphrase what Ignatius called "disordered attachments," those derailing, often subtle inner drives that can pull us away from being our best selves. To uncover what inner baggage may be weighing you down, look through other exercises and your responses so far before filling out the wheel below.

IDENTIFY YOUR INNER BAGGAGE

Rate how big your inner baggage is for each of the segments on the carousel. Shade in the areas accordingly.
0 = Total freedom to live to fulfill your purpose—that baggage weighs nothing **10** = That baggage is mighty heavy
The types of baggage illustrated here are characteristic derailers for many, but if you have another kind of baggage not listed, feel free to add or swap them out.

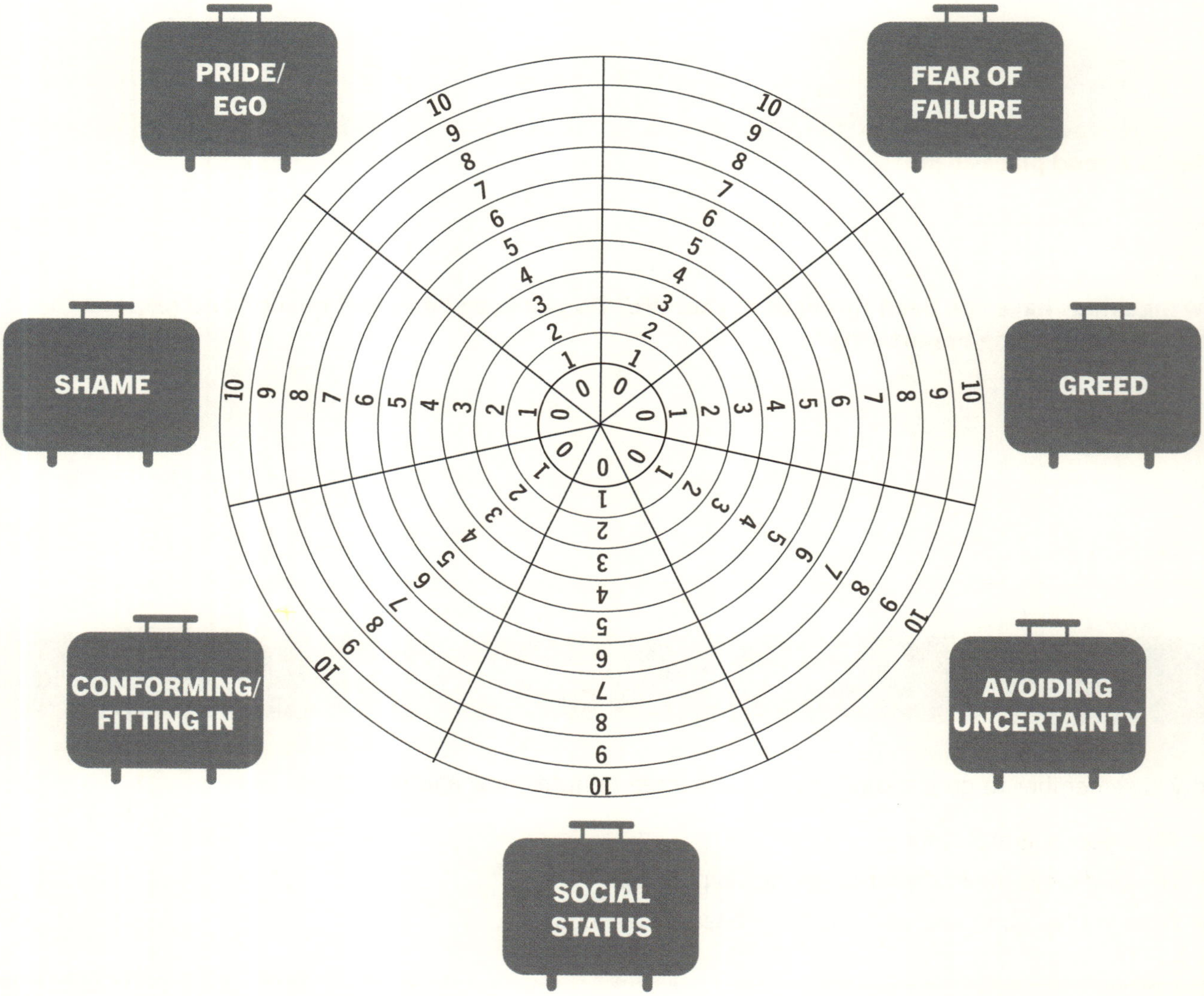

"A leader must rid him- or herself of ingrained habits, prejudices, cultural preferences, and the 'we've always done it this way' attitude—the baggage that blocks rapid adaptive responses."

TAKE ACTION

Take a look at your baggage carousel and consider which suitcases are weighing you down. Here you'll decide how to start freeing yourself. First, imagine yourself going through a day without this baggage. Then, do it!

How do these heavy suitcases weigh you down in big life decisions? Day-to-day? At home? At work? What do they cost you?

Is there one piece of baggage that, if lightened, might have a domino effect on the other baggage? This is a good place to start.

What one thing could you do in your next day of work to practice setting down your baggage?

"This journey involves identifying personal, derailing baggage that prevents the realization of full potential, especially weaknesses that manifest themselves as habitual tendencies."

DAY 12: COGNITIVE DISTORTIONS

We develop patterns of thinking, and sometimes these patterns not only distort reality, but also weigh us down. Psychologists call these unhelpful thinking patterns cognitive distortions.

In the list of common cognitive distortions below, circle or highlight any that you recognize in your own thinking patterns. It may be helpful to rate, on a scale of 0 to 10, the extent to which each of these distortions is a part of your thinking.

POLARIZED THINKING

A person who does not get a stellar performance review feels like a failure because they are used to being "the best." They think, *If I am not excellent at everything I do, I am a complete failure.*

☐

NEGATIVE MENTAL FILTERING

A learner gets a lot of positive praise for their assignment, and one criticism. The learner focuses only on the negative, discounting the positive.

☐

DISQUALIFYING THE POSITIVE

A learner gets a lot of positive praise for an assignment and decides this has no meaning, telling themselves it was luck or a mistake.

☐

OVERGENERALIZATION

A person knows that a co-worker does not particularly find them pleasant company. The person decides that it isn't just one co-worker, but rather "nobody likes me."

☐

MIND-READING

A person's supervisor has been quiet, sullen even. The person thinks it is because of them.

☐

FORTUNE-TELLING

A person has to have a difficult conversation with someone and "just knows" it will go badly. They are telling the future before it happens.

☐

"Those who have pinpointed and begun to root out their weaknesses and unhealthy attachments are building the indifference essential to ingenuity."

MAGNIFICATION

Someone is absent from a meeting or event. A person's imagination runs away with bigger and bigger ideas about what has gone wrong.

☐

PERSONALIZATION

A staff member or learner fails to perform, or there is some other perceived failure. Although this could be due to a myriad of factors, a person thinks they are solely to blame; they make their personal role bigger than it actually is.

☐

BLAMING

A mistake is made on a person's team and they receive negative feedback about their performance. They think everyone and anyone else is responsible other than them and that people are out to hurt them. They are a victim.

☐

MINIMIZATION

A person achieves a goal and has success and minimizes its importance or their accomplishment.

☐

TAKE ACTION

Choose one or two of the distortions that you rated highest and jot them down in the box below. Start to consciously pay attention to them in the next few days. When such thoughts come up, practice replacing the distorted thought with a more realistic one. This is part of a therapeutic approach to mental health called cognitive behavioral therapy.

"The pursuit of self-awareness is grounded in the reality that humans make mistakes—lots of them. But leaders go steps further: they reflect on mistakes, learn from them, and move on."

DAY 13: HANDLING SETBACKS

Read each of the dilemmas below. Pick at least one of these dilemmas that really hits you and consider how you have handled it. If time or energy allows, address all four dilemmas. One row has also been left blank for you to add your own.

DILEMMA	HOW DID I HANDLE THIS WELL?	HOW MIGHT I HAVE HANDLED THIS BETTER?	WHAT WAS IN MY CONTROL AND WHAT WASN'T?
My heart was set on a particular career or life path and a setback destroyed my plans.			
I have a vague dream of what I want to accomplish but no plan to make it happen.			
I know I can make a difference in the world, but I lack confidence in my talents and abilities.			
My circumstances keep changing for better or worse, and I must keep adapting my life plans in response.			
Add your own			

"Without the setbacks, crises, and challenges that punctuated his real life, [Loyola] might never have grappled with who he was, what he wanted, what personal resources he had, and why he had failed along the way."

REFLECTION

In *Heroic Leadership*, I explain on page 245 that "leadership is a way of living in which basic life strategies and principles reinforce one another." With that in mind, review your responses in the chart you've just completed. Which of the following constructive strategies for making high-quality decisions have you regularly used when facing dilemmas? Put a checkmark (√) beside the strategies you see evident in your past responses. Use the second column to record how you used these strategies. Put an asterisk (*) beside the strategies you wish you'd used but didn't. How might you have used them? Write your answers in the third column.

STRATEGY FOR DEALING WITH DILEMMAS	THIS IS HOW I USED THIS STRATEGY	HOW I WISH I HAD USED THIS STRATEGY
Take charge of my life		
Retreat to think and make a decision		
Control what I can about my circumstances		
Free myself from fears and unhealthy attachments		
Recognize my gut instinct or listen to my heart		
Talk to a friend who listens to and supports me without telling me what to do		
Stay consistent		

TAKE ACTION

Consider the strategies you used. How might you enhance your use of them in the future? How might you encourage others in your workplace to use these strategies?

Consider the strategies you wished you had used. What small step might you take to incorporate one of these strategies the next time you face a dilemma?

"The indifferent Jesuit liberates himself to choose strategies driven by one motive only: achieving his long-term goal of serving God by helping souls."

DAY 14: A GRETZKY AUDIT

Hockey legend Wayne Gretzky said, "You miss 100% of the shots you don't take." The clever quip encourages us to cultivate a positive rather than fearful attitude toward the opportunities life presents to try new approaches. Chapter 10 in *Heroic Leadership* addresses risk-taking ("taking shots") in leadership.

In this exercise, you have the opportunity to reflect on risk-taking in your life or workplace.

	IN THESE LAST FEW MONTHS . . .	IN THE NEXT SIX MONTHS . . .	IN THE NEXT THREE YEARS . . .
What shots have you taken?			
What shots has your team taken?			
What shots has your organization taken?			
What shots would be interesting?			
What shots do you want to take?			

NOTE: If you can't come up with any examples at all amid a world that is changing so much around us, that might indicate that the way you are doing everything is 100% perfect (not likely!). It's more likely that this is a worrisome indicator that you are too risk-averse and you are not being ingenious enough in your approach to a changing world.

"The end of risk-taking almost ended the Jesuits."

DAY 15: PRACTICING INGENIOUS DECISIONS

Educators and professionals work in high-pressure environments that regularly force them to make critical decisions with limited resources, often in short time frames. They routinely face social, moral, and ethical dilemmas as they navigate tough choices.

For the next exercise, imagine a workplace decision that you would find difficult. You might come up with your own—for example, a decision from your past experience that you are not sure about, or you might imagine a decision you've watched someone else make and you were glad you were not in their shoes. Or you might choose from one of the following scenarios:

- Allocate substantial resources to projects and programs that improve lives without sufficient financial ROI.
- Forge new partnerships with newly established technology companies.
- Either engage others such as resource services, administrators, or parents when an employee or a student is having difficulties, or deal with the problem yourself.
- Adjust activities to meet the needs of students, customers, or clients in ways that are not necessarily the organization's or institute's first priority.
- Navigate relationships between staff and colleagues who have conflicting priorities such as curriculum design and the department's strategic plan.
- Encourage employees to either go home at the end of their shift or stay late, or do one or the other yourself, knowing that leaving induces feelings of abandoning the people who remain.
- Either spend time keeping up-to-date with policy in emergent, critical situations, or focus on the tasks at hand.

"Employees who once might have been reprimanded for not clearing decisions with managers before making them will today more likely be penalized for not showing enough initiative."

Imagine yourself about to make your chosen decision. Draw upon past experiences as much as you can to make this imagined scenario as realistic as possible. Visualize yourself in the situation. Imagine yourself making this decision in a healthy, ingenious way.

Where are you?

What time of day is it?

Who is there with you?

What is happening around you?

What thoughts are going through your mind?

What emotions do you feel?

What are your fears and worries?

What are your hopes?

If your core values are a violin, what strings does this decision pluck?

Do you need to act fast, or can you take some time?

What are your core values, and how do they guide your actions?

What are your typical unfreedoms? Imagine how you will respond without your usual baggage weighing you down.

Imagine yourself, as fully as you can, going through the process of making a decision and then, with your baggage aside, declare or ingeniously act upon your decision.

"Leaders imagine an inspiring future and strive to shape it rather than passively watching the future happen around them."

DAY 16: MORAL DILEMMA

In this exercise you will apply the ingenious approach for decision-making to a moral dilemma in the workplace. The aim is to practice relating your core values to a common dilemma. What are the challenges, how will you make the final decision, and what will that decision be?

THE DILEMMA

Imagine that you lead a small but dynamic team of individuals working on a project with a tight deadline and a number of deliverables due at the end of the month. One team member has not done his share of work, has let critical deadlines pass, and has talked negatively about the project behind your back. This has occurred even though you have spoken to him before about his attitude and placed him on a personal improvement plan.

Even so, you know that any loss of staff right now would sink the project. In addition, you have mentored this person and feel personally responsible for his success. He is a single parent who is also looking after an elderly parent. Today, another team member complained about him to you confidentially.

1. What decision will you make about this teammate and why?
2. What do you imagine the effects of your actions to be?
3. How do personal values and organizational values affect decision-making?

YOUR VALUES AND PURPOSE

Review your core values and greater purpose (Days 4 and 5); jot some notes in the box below so you have these thoughts at hand.

Review your organization's mission and values and make notes here.

"The pace of societal and corporate change is accelerating, and whether in their personal or professional lives, individuals are forced to make more decisions and make them faster—with less guidance, incomplete information, and few relevant precedents."

OTHERS' CORE VALUES

On page 176 in *Heroic Leadership* I describe "love-driven" leadership as "the vision to see each person's talent, potential, and dignity; the courage, passion, and commitment to unlock that potential; and the resulting loyalty and mutual support that energize and unite teams."

With this in mind, consider the viewpoints of others in the scenario (e.g., clients, team members, administrators). We have included an additional space for other stakeholders that may be particular to your situation. Your goal is to begin unpacking how your decision affects others, and the potentially conflicting core values that are implicated in the various options.

STAKEHOLDER	WHAT OUTCOME DO THEY WANT? WHAT VALUES ARE DRIVING THESE NEEDS AND DESIRES?	WHAT ASSUMPTIONS ARE YOU MAKING? WHAT DON'T YOU KNOW ABOUT THIS STAKEHOLDER'S WANTS, NEEDS, OR VALUES?
CLIENT		
PROBLEMATIC TEAM MEMBER		
OTHER TEAM MEMBERS		
DIRECTOR/DEAN/ ADMINISTRATION		
OTHER		

"No one perceives others accurately without first achieving healthy self-regard. Appreciate your potential, unique talent, and fundamental human dignity. Then see others, their birthright nothing less than the very same human dignity."

POTENTIAL DECISIONS AND THEIR CONSEQUENCES

Below are a series of potential decisions appropriate for this scenario. One row is left blank should you perceive a different potential decision not listed.

For each scenario, first consider how you might mitigate negative consequences that could occur as a result of your decision. Then, consider your core values, your organization's values, and those of all the stakeholders. What values are in conflict?

Take, for example, fairness, integrity, care for the organization, employees, clients, and excellence. Does the potential decision prioritize some values over others, and if so, how?

POTENTIAL SCENARIO	POTENTIAL CONSEQUENCES	VALUES IN CONFLICT AND VALUES PRIORITIZED
You discuss the situation with the problem employee, and they promise to correct their behavior.		
You discuss the situation with the problem employee and decide to end his employment.		
You reassign tasks on the team so that the least damage is done to the project.		
You replace the problem employee with someone from another team.		
You do nothing for the time being to get through the end of the month.		
Other potential decision:		

"Early Jesuit recruits discovered the power of explicitly naming their values: this is who I am, this is what I stand for, this is what I want."

MAKE A DECISION

Review your responses above. Take some time for reflection or prayer to practice discernment before making a decision.

REFLECTION

How does your decision relate to your core values? Your organization's values?

Some decisions we make are not obviously right or wrong. How might you prepare for events down the line that could suggest an alternative decision would have been preferable?

"The job of Jesuit managers was not to persuade recruits what to do but to equip them with the skills to discern on their own what needed to be done."

LOVE

Leaders should "love" their team members? *Really?* Truth be told, I did not wander the hallways of J.P. Morgan telling colleagues that I loved them! And yet, I did my best to follow the wisdom of Ignatius of Loyola, who said that love ought to manifest itself in deeds, not words.

So, what kinds of deeds are we talking about? Philosophers remind us that loving means "willing and working for 'the good' of another." And, with that simple insight, our role as "loving leaders" locks into focus: as a parent or teacher, I love those in my care by striving for their "good"—namely, that they learn and grow, remain healthy, develop a moral compass, and, over time, reach their full potential. And as a loving manager, mentor, or chief executive, I should strive for similar outcomes, namely, that team members develop their skills, learn new things, feel challenged, enjoy opportunities to advance, be treated with respect, and reach their fullest potential. Sheryl Sandberg, the former COO of Facebook, indirectly captured the essence of loving leadership when she talked about leadership in terms of making other people better as a result of you being present.

As explored in chapter 8 in *Heroic Leadership*, the transformative power of this leadership style is clear: we ourselves become more generous, more effective leaders who focus on making colleagues better, not on looking good ourselves. Consequently, our team members continually develop their talent and, as teams attain full potential, the whole organization's performance invariably improves.

Although loving leadership might seem an unfamiliar notion, this week's exercises will undoubtedly reveal that you've experienced it often. You'll reflect on the managers or teachers who have most impacted you, and their winning behaviors will likely form a portrait of loving leadership in action. You'll also explore how closely love-driven leadership aligns with another rich leadership model: servant leadership. By week's end, you will have developed a clearer strategy for manifesting love-driven leadership in your own life and work.

"In short, love-driven leadership is the vision to see each person's talent, potential, and dignity; the courage, passion, and commitment to unlock that potential; and the resulting loyalty and mutual support that energize and unite teams."

DAY 17: LOVE-DRIVEN LEADERSHIP

In the box below, jot down a list of some qualities and behaviors that would characterize love-driven leadership in a workplace. Don't overthink it! You've been a leader and manager, or you've had the experience of being led or managed. Recall behaviors that distinguished a manager who seemed to want the best for everyone on the team, and who wanted each person to develop to their fullest potential.

WHAT MAKES A GOOD MANAGER?

Use the chart below to think about the good managers you have known. What qualities, attitudes, or behaviors won your respect and cooperation? Then think about the managers you have encountered who did not win your respect. What did they do wrong? Why didn't they win your respect?

	MANAGERS WHO WON MY RESPECT	MANAGERS WHO DID NOT WIN MY RESPECT
Personal qualities and character traits		
How they approached the world, work, and people		
What actions they took or did not take		
Other attributes that come to mind		

Look at the list of qualities that you associate with love-driven leadership. Compare this list to your chart about managers. Circle any attributes in your chart that are similar or appear in your list. Then, underline or highlight any qualities of managers who did not win your respect.

"Individuals perform best when they are respected, valued, and trusted by those who genuinely care for their well-being."

DAY 18: LOVE IN YOUR WORK LIFE

Revisit your My Life and Career Journey timeline from Day 2 and look back at the key moments you've identified.

How did support from others influence those moments? Consider especially support you received in the workplace.

How did a lack of loving leadership influence your key events?

How did your own loving behavior influence those key moments?

How did your lack of loving behavior influence your key events?

How has love been important to your work life and beyond?

"Those who treat others with respect and love are leading the way to environments of greater love than fear, where many more people will enjoy the chance to achieve their full human potential."

DAY 19: LIFE'S OPPORTUNITIES FOR LOVE-DRIVEN LEADERSHIP

Before beginning this workbook, you may never have thought of love-driven leadership, much less that it applied to your own life. But with a little reflection, it will become increasingly clear that you are already a love-driven leader in many ways, and every day of your life is presenting opportunities for love-driven leadership.

Recall the definitional ideas that we've introduced about what "loving" genuinely means: it's about wanting and working for what's good for other people in your life; it's about making others better as a result of your presence; it's about becoming a servant leader who helps people reach their potential.

With these ideas in mind, think about where you interact regularly with other people: in family life, at work, at religious services, when meeting friends, or in the community. Jot down some of the many ways in which you are exhibiting love-driven leadership in these environments:

An appropriate love of oneself is also part of a healthy life. Think about your work and other life commitments and jot down how these are also opportunities for you to develop your talents, become a better person, and reach your full potential:

"When love-driven leadership takes root on a widespread basis, it energizes performances and creates unique bonds of team unity."

DAY 20: ENCOURAGING LOVING LEADERSHIP IN YOUR WORKPLACE

Before starting this exercise, read through your responses for Days 17, 18, and 19, paying attention to what love-driven leadership looks like in the workplace.

Consider your workplace or the other settings within which you regularly interact with people. Think about your colleagues, friends, the clerks at the grocery store, everyone. What behaviors, words, and attitudes have you noticed in them that are manifestations of love-driven leadership?

TAKE ACTION

How might you further encourage these attributes of loving leadership in your staff or colleagues? Consider whether there are particular times or contexts in which these behaviors and attitudes are more prevalent; what encouraging words or actions you might use; and how the role you play can be used to model or promote loving leadership.

I will encourage loving leadership by:

"For teachers, parents, managers, coaches, mentors, and friends, expressing love through deeds, not words, means helping others bring their potential to fruition."

TAKE ACTION

What might you be doing or saying that detracts from loving leadership? What benefits might you see if you stopped these love-discouraging actions and words? Are there particular times or contexts in which these behaviors and attitudes are less prevalent in your workplace? What role do you play in these scenarios?

I will stop diminishing loving leadership in my workplace, school, or community by:

REFLECTION

How might your workplace, school, or community change if you encouraged loving leadership in your staff/colleagues?

STILL DOING YOUR DAILY *EXAMEN*? IF SO—GOOD FOR YOU! IT'S CHALLENGING TO MAINTAIN A NEW ROUTINE. IF NOT, TAKE A FEW MINUTES TO PERFORM IT NOW!

"By relentlessly urging their teams to a generous, wide ranging vision of love, Loyola and his cofounders tapped an invigorating leadership principle."

DAY 21: WITH OR WITHOUT YOU

In the space below, describe how and why your colleagues are better as a result of your presence. You might consider this prompt generally, or you can consider specific people or roles you work with. Be honest with yourself.

TAKE ACTION

On a scale of 0–10, how satisfied are you with your response to the prompt above?

What can you start doing to be a more love-driven leader?

"Heroic leadership invites people to assess their daily impact, to refocus if necessary, and to articulate the leadership mark they want to make."

THOSE YOU SERVE

Being a loving leader ultimately means transcending yourself and your own interests in order to serve the needs of your:

- Students and customers
- Community
- Stakeholders
- Family members

Again, be honest with yourself in describing how your students, customers, community, stakeholders and family are better as a result of your presence.

TAKE ACTION

On a scale of 0–10, how satisfied are you with your response?

"Leader-managers today commit to making similar investments in their subordinates, not out of duty or some vague desire to be nice, but out of what might be called enlightened love."

DAY 22: A SERVANT LEADERSHIP AUDIT

In *The Servant as Leader*, Robert K. Greenleaf pioneered the idea that true leaders don't seek to be served, but serve others by helping them flourish. Greenleaf's vision dovetails beautifully with love-driven leadership. Below are some of the qualities that Greenleaf associates with servant leadership; assess how well you've been a servant/loving leader.

DO THOSE YOU SERVE . . .	EVIDENCE OF MY SERVANT LEADERSHIP
Grow as a person?	
Become healthier mentally, spiritually, physically?	
Become wiser, freer, more autonomous?	
Become more likely to be servants themselves?	

REFLECTION

Given the above, what unspoken, perhaps even subconscious mentality do you bring to your life as a leader? To what extent do you operate as if others are there to serve you? On the other hand, to what extent do you serve them?

"Total victory demands more than total commitment: it requires going further than wholehearted service."

DAY 23: LOVE-DRIVEN VISION

In the chart below, write the roles of each person on your team. Then, identify their talents and potential and what you as a love-driven leader could do to unlock this potential.

ROLE OF EACH PERSON ON YOUR TEAM	PROFESSIONAL TALENTS	PROFESSIONAL POTENTIAL	WHAT COULD A LOVE-DRIVEN LEADER DO TO UNLOCK THIS POTENTIAL?
YOUR JOB/ROLE:			

Based on the chart above, write a sentence or two summarizing how your team would function and excel if everyone was fully supported.

"In short, love-driven leadership is the vision to see each person's talent, potential and dignity, and the courage, passion, and commitment to unlock that potential."

HEROISM

Last week's exercises began sharpening our focus on a "North Star" for life and leadership choices: we are here to be loving leaders. We want family, friends, team members, and customers to flourish and reach their full potential. This week's exercises will focus on a complementary theme: what does it mean to lead heroically, to strive for excellence as we devote ourselves to purposes greater than self.

As kids, our heroes might have been sports stars or celebrities. But our vision of heroism undoubtedly matures as we do. Instead of idolizing those who chase fame, we start admiring parents, teachers, and others who sacrifice fame (and time and money). These people are heroic because they transcend themselves and their egos, serving missions that inspire their allegiance, excellence, and imagination.

Jesuits, for example, often encapsulate their ultimate purpose as a lifelong pursuit of plans and dreams that are "AMDG," a Latin acronym that translates as either "For God's Greater Glory" or "For the Greater Glory of God." (The point: I'm here on earth to work toward God's greater glory, not for my own honor and glory.)

Most of us are not Jesuits, of course, so this week will prompt us to recall (or articulate anew) our own heroic purposes, consistent with our spirituality and ideals, whether that entails deeply religious aspirations or humanistic ideals like striving for the common good or giving more love than I receive.

Sometimes, the real challenge is not in articulating a purpose but living it amid each day's messy reality. We may drift into "split-life-ism," that de-energizing, soul-deadening lifestyle where we don't feel able to bring our deeply held values to our work. Days 24 and 27 will challenge us to find the everyday opportunities and courage to avoid "split-life-ism."

Days 28–30 will be capstone exercises. You'll weave your learnings into a personal credo, a statement of how you now want to lead. While pondering your credo, please celebrate all that you've discovered over these weeks. Congratulations on your commitment to lead heroically!

"Heroic leaders seek to shape the future rather than passively endure whatever unfolds."

DAY 24: DO WHAT YOU'RE DOING

Chapter 9 in *Heroic Leadership* notes that "excellence doesn't occur accidentally." Rather, heroic leaders strive to become their best selves by developing fully their gifts and talents.

Use the exercise below to assess how purposefully you strive for excellence. In the first column, jot down the key tasks, duties, and responsibilities you do regularly in your job. In the second column, think objectively about what excellence looks like in that task. Don't evaluate your own performance, but rather consider what your organization wants and needs for each task. Be specific. Then, in the last column, rate your own performance on a scale of 0 to 10. How well do you exhibit excellence in each task?

KEY TASKS	EXCELLENCE	YOUR RATING (0–10)

REFLECTION

Overall, in what ways are you exhibiting excellence at work?

Based on the things you can control (e.g., behavior, engagement, further learning), what can you commit to doing now that would boost your excellence at work?

"Excellence—like the leadership that engenders it—is no timeless plateau that once attained is never forfeited."

DAY 25: HEROIC MISSION

In *Heroic Leadership*, we learn that organizational mission statements don't mean very much unless they are embraced and lived by team members: "Company mission statements don't take root simply because they've been elegantly worded. They take root when subordinates see managers take a personal interest in the mission" (p. 19).

With that in mind, use this exercise to articulate your organization's ambitions in ways that speak to the part of you, and your team, that really wants to be challenged and to be involved in something much larger than yourselves—something you consider noble and worthy.

What is your organization's mission?

What are the values inherent in the mission?

What can you find in your organization's mission that resonates with your own sense of mission in the world? What connections to your core values can you find/make?

TAKE ACTION

Review your responses to the above questions and consider how the mission overlaps with your (and your team's) core values, purpose, and motivations.

What are two ways that you might remind yourself of these connections and/or communicate them to your team?

1.

2.

"[This is] a key difference between heroic and run-of-the-mill organizations: widely dispersed leadership in which each person considers, accepts, shapes, and transforms a general mission into a personal one."

DAY 26: FOLLOW THROUGH

On page 294 in *Heroic Leadership*, I explain that "[heroic leaders] see the wisdom and value in the *examen* and commit to it—the daily, self-reflective habit of refocusing on priorities and extracting lessons from successes and failures."

In conjunction with your ongoing practice of the *examen*, take some time to reflect on your priorities. What major life priorities do you seem to have trouble tackling?

What aren't you doing that you know you need to do?

Heroic leaders set lofty life goals, whether personal, professional, or spiritual. What are yours? If it will help, continue your My Life and Career Journey timeline from Day 2 into the future, marking key moments and milestones that you'd like to bring to fruition.

"What springs from within makes the difference between talking the talk and walking the walk."

The Spiritual Exercises of St. Ignatius of Loyola are not rules to be read or studied, but rather "actions to be done" (p. 114). Look at your life priorities and your lofty goals. Break those lofty goals into bite-sized, doable action pieces with shorter time frames. What would success look like this week? What action steps might you take to get up the mountain?

TAKE ACTION

Having a mission, a purpose, and a strategy is not the hard part. Following through is.
Take a look at what you just wrote. Look at your purpose, values, and lofty goals. Decide on one core thing you need to do. Write it down. And then . . . do it!

I need to . . .

Who might help hold you accountable for what you want to improve/achieve?

Write a few names of people who might be good mentors. Then, take the step and ask them to hold you accountable.

"The self-awareness accomplished during the Exercises is a prelude to action."

DAY 27: EVERYDAY COURAGE

Courage is sometimes associated with grand acts of bravery in extraordinary circumstances. There is plenty of that kind of courage in education, business, and family and community life. But *Heroic Leadership* also emphasizes that "leaders have the courage and the will to keep going" to take on everyday challenges (p. 272). Use the following chart to collect evidence that this kind of everyday courage is not only possible in your workplace, but already present. Feel free to focus only on the aspects of everyday courage that resonate most strongly with you.

ASPECT OF EVERYDAY COURAGE	EVIDENCE THAT I HAVE EXHIBITED THIS KIND OF COURAGE IN THE LAST MONTH	EVIDENCE THAT MY COLLEAGUES HAVE EXHIBITED THIS KIND OF COURAGE IN THE LAST MONTH
Taking the risk to try something you're afraid of trying		
Saying what should be said even if you fear it might cost you		
Persevering in pursuing something important, despite doubts about whether it can work out		
Striving for excellence when it's more comfortable to settle for less		
The quiet courage to get up and try again tomorrow in the face of adversity		
The courage to be your authentic self		

"[Heroes] demonstrate the courage, nobility, and greatness of heart to pursue a personal sense of *magis*, to keep themselves pointed toward goals that enhance them as people."

REFLECTION

When you look at the evidence of everyday courage in your life or workplace, what aspect(s) do you (and your colleagues) do particularly well? How might you celebrate this courage to fortify your spirit and those around you?

Is there an aspect of everyday courage that you would like to cultivate? How might you add this priority to your daily *examen* or other personal strategies?

"Love-driven Jesuits worked with passion and courage, whether teaching teenagers or confronting colonialists who abused Indigenous peoples in Latin America."

DAY 28: TRANSCENDENCE

According to *Heroic Leadership*, "Real leaders—real heroes—find fulfillment, meaning, and even success by shifting their gaze beyond self-interest and serving others" (p. 292). Indeed, the *Heroic Leadership* approach brings the invigorating joy of pursuing a transcendent vision of self-leadership. That is, we transcend our old self to become our best possible self; we transcend the way it's always been done before to imagine new pathways for ourselves and our organizations; and, above all, we transcend our selfish ego-needs to find fulfillment in serving others, the common good, or the highest calling of our religious beliefs.

Review your responses in this workbook. In the space below, note all the hopeful possibilities you've identified for transcending yourself: toward new ways of being, thinking, and doing; toward purpose beyond self; toward doing and being more than you once thought possible.

Organize your learnings and insights further by aligning them with each of the four pillars, according to the prompts that follow.

Self-awareness: I'm transcending shallow or unreflective self-concepts to understand myself and my values in newer, deeper, more insightful ways, as, for example . . .

Ingenuity: I'm transcending the fears, hesitations, and other inner baggage that has held me back from being adaptive, creative, and from considering new approaches in my life or work, such as . . .

Love: I'm transcending self-centeredness to be more focused on lifting up, empowering, and nurturing the potential of those around me, for example, by . . .

Heroism: I'm transcending narrow, materialistic, or short-term goals in life for a calling or a loftier sense of purpose, such as . . .

"[The Jesuits give] each person an opportunity to enlarge himself by contributing meaningfully to an enterprise greater than his own interests."

TAKE ACTION

Write an action statement to crystallize your commitment to make a more transcendent approach to self-leadership.

I will . . .

"Heroes lift themselves up and make themselves greater by pursuing something greater than their own self-interest."

DAY 29: DIALOGUE

This workbook is meant to be a dialogue of sorts—an invitation and sometimes a challenge. At this stage, take a moment to consider all you've learned and how it connects to your:

- Current understandings
- Past learnings concerning leadership
- Personal experiences

List three ways *The Heroic Leadership Workbook* aligns with your past learnings and experiences.

-
-
-

List three ideas in *The Heroic Leadership Workbook* that align with the wisdom you've gleaned from your life experiences or spiritual tradition.

-
-
-

List three ways *The Heroic Leadership Workbook* has challenged your thinking.

-
-
-

List one or two things in *The Heroic Leadership Workbook* that you have shared or will share with others.

-
-

"Deeply rooted in the rhythm of Jesuit life was the belief that personal growth and development were possible, that those attempting to 'run at full speed towards perfection' were not stuck on a treadmill but moving forward."

DAY 30: A NEW LEADER'S CREDO

On page 21 in *Heroic Leadership*, I write: "If all leadership is first self-leadership that springs from personal beliefs and attitudes, then each person must first decide what personal leadership legacy he or she wants to leave behind."

This workbook ends, then, with what might be called a new leader's credo. As a result of decades of laboring alongside colleagues of every (and no) spiritual tradition, I am convinced that there is at least one thing almost all of us share in common: the desire to rid our culture of mean-spirited, self-absorbed leadership and replace it with the kind of principled, effective, great-spirited leadership that our wonderful yet troubled world desperately needs and deserves. And the best place to begin is to model that style of leadership ourselves.

This exercise invites you to commit, in writing, to specific actions to bring this vision of leadership vibrantly alive in your own pursuits. To begin, first look back at the self-awareness section of this workbook, Days 3 through 9, and have your core values and purpose fresh in your mind.

TAKE ACTION

You are called to lead, to point out a way and influence others, whether you are currently doing so as a student, parent, parish leader, or corporate manager. But you can't lead anyone else if you can't lead yourself. Complete each of the following prompts, drawn from the four pillars, for the purpose of articulating your own leadership vision.

1. Self-awareness: I commit to live my life every day according to my foremost values in these ways . . .

"The modern-day leader who maintains a self-reflective instinct, like the Jesuits who did so nearly five centuries ago, avoids the worst leadership tragedy of all: waking up one morning plagued by the distressing question, 'What have I been doing with my life for the last year, last five, last thirty?'"

TAKE ACTION

!

2. **Ingenuity: In a rapidly changing world, I acknowledge that leadership involves helping create the future. I resolve to work hard to free myself from my fears of ____________________ as well as my inner baggage about ____________________ so that I am ready at all times to optimistically create a future that is ____________________.**

3. **Love: I will walk the world with my eyes and heart open to the joys and suffering around me. I commit to loving my colleagues and the community we serve by . . .**

4. **Heroism: I commit to transcending myself to serve a purpose greater than myself. Our challenges are great, and we need heroic leaders to help surmount them. I acknowledge that I am presented with leadership opportunities every day with the people in front of me right now, with the problems I am asked to solve, with my attitude in the face of adversity. I commit to stretching myself so that I can become a more heroic leader by embracing opportunities such as ____________________ that are coming to me every day. I commit to:**

"More important than when each person discovers defining life principles is making the commitment to pursue them. Whether these life principles are discovered early or late in life, the commitment to measure life choices against them is crucial."

MY NEW LEADER CREDO

Based on your statements above, put together your own personal new leader credo that resonates with you and represents a commitment you can take pride in and be challenged by.

"Infinitely more valuable than the plan, product, and capital the Jesuits so obviously lacked was what the founders did have: uncompromising commitment to a unique way of working and living, to a life that integrated four leadership principles—self-awareness, ingenuity, love, and heroism."

ACKNOWLEDGMENTS

Great organizational leadership is a team sport, not a solo act. I'm deeply grateful, therefore, to this workbook's "leadership team." I am blessed to work with Loyola Press again, where Gary Jansen, Joe Paprocki, and Maura Poston brought their impressive authorial expertise and wise touches to the text.

Readers who may want to undertake these workbook exercises as part of a cohort, in a university-credentialed certificate program, have two wonderful opportunities to do so:

- I'm grateful to Dennis Lanham, Robert Brancatelli, and colleagues at Santa Clara University's Silicon Valley Executive Center, who run an online leadership program based on this workbook—a program targeted particularly at graduates of Jesuit institutions and those who work in them.
- And I owe a huge debt of gratitude to OpusVi, where Andrew Malley, Julie DeLoia, and colleagues first imagined and proposed the *Heroic Leadership in Healthcare* workbook, brought it to fruition, and now offer the program regularly to those in healthcare professions. This workbook would not exist without their initiative. To my great fortune, Judy Wearing, OpusVi's "Lead Learning Architect," was my trusted guide (and a delightful partner!) in developing the exercises that comprise this workbook. She is exactly what her job title suggests: someone who knew how to translate a book like *Heroic Leadership* into a learning journey that is practical and concrete, while remaining true to a vision that leadership is a profound undertaking.

BIBLIOGRAPHY

Greenleaf, Robert K. *The Servant as Leader.* South Orange, NJ: The Greenleaf Center for Servant Leadership, 2015.

Lowney, Chris. *Heroic Leadership: Best Practices from a 450-Year-Old Company That Changed the World.* Chicago: Loyola Press, 2003.

Puhl, Louis J., SJ. *The Spiritual Exercises of Saint Ignatius.* 2nd ed. Chicago: Loyola Press, 2021.

NOTES

NOTES

NOTES

NOTES

NOTES

NOTES

NOTES

NOTES